An account of the Fair Intellectual-Club in Edinburgh: in a letter to a honourable member of an Athenian Society there. By a young lady, the secretary of the club.

M. C.

ECCO
PRINT EDITIONS

An account of the Fair Intellectual-Club in Edinburgh: in a letter to a honourable member of
an Athenian Society there. By a young lady, the secretary of the club.
M. C.
ESTCID: T073473
Reproduction from British Library
Signed at end: M.C.
Edinburgh : printed by J. M'Euan and Company, and to be sold at the said J. M'Euan's shop in Edinburgh, and T. Cox in London, 1720.
[8],32p. ; 4°

Eighteenth Century
Collections Online
Print Editions

Gale ECCO Print Editions

Relive history with *Eighteenth Century Collections Online*, now available in print for the independent historian and collector. This series includes the most significant English-language and foreign-language works printed in Great Britain during the eighteenth century, and is organized in seven different subject areas including literature and language; medicine, science, and technology; and religion and philosophy. The collection also includes thousands of important works from the Americas.

The eighteenth century has been called "The Age of Enlightenment." It was a period of rapid advance in print culture and publishing, in world exploration, and in the rapid growth of science and technology – all of which had a profound impact on the political and cultural landscape. At the end of the century the American Revolution, French Revolution and Industrial Revolution, perhaps three of the most significant events in modern history, set in motion developments that eventually dominated world political, economic, and social life.

In a groundbreaking effort, Gale initiated a revolution of its own: digitization of epic proportions to preserve these invaluable works in the largest online archive of its kind. Contributions from major world libraries constitute over 175,000 original printed works. Scanned images of the actual pages, rather than transcriptions, recreate the works *as they first appeared.*

Now for the first time, these high-quality digital scans of original works are available via print-on-demand, making them readily accessible to libraries, students, independent scholars, and readers of all ages.

For our initial release we have created seven robust collections to form one the world's most comprehensive catalogs of 18th century works.

Initial Gale ECCO Print Editions collections include:

History and Geography
Rich in titles on English life and social history, this collection spans the world as it was known to eighteenth-century historians and explorers. Titles include a wealth of travel accounts and diaries, histories of nations from throughout the world, and maps and charts of a world that was still being discovered. Students of the War of American Independence will find fascinating accounts from the British side of conflict.

Social Science

Delve into what it was like to live during the eighteenth century by reading the first-hand accounts of everyday people, including city dwellers and farmers, businessmen and bankers, artisans and merchants, artists and their patrons, politicians and their constituents. Original texts make the American, French, and Industrial revolutions vividly contemporary.

Medicine, Science and Technology

Medical theory and practice of the 1700s developed rapidly, as is evidenced by the extensive collection, which includes descriptions of diseases, their conditions, and treatments. Books on science and technology, agriculture, military technology, natural philosophy, even cookbooks, are all contained here.

Literature and Language

Western literary study flows out of eighteenth-century works by Alexander Pope, Daniel Defoe, Henry Fielding, Frances Burney, Denis Diderot, Johann Gottfried Herder, Johann Wolfgang von Goethe, and others. Experience the birth of the modern novel, or compare the development of language using dictionaries and grammar discourses.

Religion and Philosophy

The Age of Enlightenment profoundly enriched religious and philosophical understanding and continues to influence present-day thinking. Works collected here include masterpieces by David Hume, Immanuel Kant, and Jean-Jacques Rousseau, as well as religious sermons and moral debates on the issues of the day, such as the slave trade. The Age of Reason saw conflict between Protestantism and Catholicism transformed into one between faith and logic -- a debate that continues in the twenty-first century.

Law and Reference

This collection reveals the history of English common law and Empire law in a vastly changing world of British expansion. Dominating the legal field is the *Commentaries of the Law of England* by Sir William Blackstone, which first appeared in 1765. Reference works such as almanacs and catalogues continue to educate us by revealing the day-to-day workings of society.

Fine Arts

The eighteenth-century fascination with Greek and Roman antiquity followed the systematic excavation of the ruins at Pompeii and Herculaneum in southern Italy; and after 1750 a neoclassical style dominated all artistic fields. The titles here trace developments in mostly English-language works on painting, sculpture, architecture, music, theater, and other disciplines. Instructional works on musical instruments, catalogs of art objects, comic operas, and more are also included.

The BiblioLife Network

This project was made possible in part by the BiblioLife Network (BLN), a project aimed at addressing some of the huge challenges facing book preservationists around the world. The BLN includes libraries, library networks, archives, subject matter experts, online communities and library service providers. We believe every book ever published should be available as a high-quality print reproduction; printed on-demand anywhere in the world. This insures the ongoing accessibility of the content and helps generate sustainable revenue for the libraries and organizations that work to preserve these important materials.

The following book is in the "public domain" and represents an authentic reproduction of the text as printed by the original publisher. While we have attempted to accurately maintain the integrity of the original work, there are sometimes problems with the original work or the micro-film from which the books were digitized. This can result in minor errors in reproduction. Possible imperfections include missing and blurred pages, poor pictures, markings and other reproduction issues beyond our control. Because this work is culturally important, we have made it available as part of our commitment to protecting, preserving, and promoting the world's literature.

GUIDE TO FOLD-OUTS MAPS and OVERSIZED IMAGES

The book you are reading was digitized from microfilm captured over the past thirty to forty years. Years after the creation of the original microfilm, the book was converted to digital files and made available in an online database.

In an online database, page images do not need to conform to the size restrictions found in a printed book. When converting these images back into a printed bound book, the page sizes are standardized in ways that maintain the detail of the original. For large images, such as fold-out maps, the original page image is split into two or more pages

Guidelines used to determine how to split the page image follows:

• Some images are split vertically; large images require vertical and horizontal splits.
• For horizontal splits, the content is split left to right.
• For vertical splits, the content is split from top to bottom.
• For both vertical and horizontal splits, the image is processed from top left to bottom right.

AN
ACCOUNT
OF THE
Fair Intellectual-Club
In *EDINBURGH:*
IN A
LETTER
To a Honourable Member
OF AN
ATHENIAN SOCIETY there.

By a young LADY, the SECRETARY of the CLUB.

NATURE, *who gave, till She could give no more,*
On WOMAN *lavish'd all Her precious Store,*
Who now courts solid and substantial Praise,
Nor values Beauty, wedded to a Fine
Her MIND *peculiar Ornaments desires,*
And Vertues proper to her SEX *requires.*

ROW's CALL.

Enter'd in Stationer's-Hall

EDINBURGH,
Printed by J. M'EUEN and COMPANY, and to be sold at the said J M'Euen's
Shop in *Edinburgh,* and T Cox at the *Amsterdam* Coffee-H le near the Royal Ex-
change in *London* 1720   Price One Shilling.

[   ]

An Advertisement to the Readers,

By Appointment of the Club.

THO' few Papers have been lately publiſhed, in this Place, that ſtand more in Need of a *Preface* to uſher them into the World, the LADIES concern'd in the following LETTER are not ſo Formal as to prefix a faſhionable *Apology* for it, nor Silly enough to court the *Readers* favour by the vulgar Arts.

WE think it may be ſufficient to inform the Pub-lick, that, after the happy Commencement of our CLUB, two Years paſt ere we were diſcovered by any Mortal. So ſecretly and cautiouſly did we manage our Affairs, that twas impoſſible for others to have found us out, if we had not reveal'd our ſelves. The

Honour-

[   ]

Honourable Gentleman, who was firſt privy to our *Conſtitution,* had remain'd as great a Stranger as his Neighbours, if one of our own Number had not betray'd us. But who can blame our Siſter? She had a generous Motive to make the Revelation. Reaſon might well quit the Field, when that almighty pleaſing Paſſion took place. What will Love not do? Love, they ſay, can break thro' brazen Gates, and Iron Bars. How then, cou'd our Siſter keep ſo innocent a Secret from her beſt Friend? What elſe wou'd all of us have done in the like Circumſtances?

> *The Strong, the Brave, the Vertuous and the Wiſe,*
> *Sink in the ſoft Captivity together.*

ADDISON'S CATO.

Yet that generous Gentleman conceal'd our *Club* above three Months from his moſt intimate Companions, and, we believe, wou'd have had the Vertue to keep the Secret for ever, if his Arguments had not prevail'd on us to entertain his Brethren of an *Athenian Society* in Town with an Account of the Original and preſent Conſtitution of our *Club.* When we were diſpos'd to do ſo, we oblig'd our Secretary, who ſhou'd have been the laſt in expoſing us, to ſuffer the Pain of writing it, as a juſt Puniſhment for her Indiſcretion. Accordingly ſhe wrote the Hiſtory in a Letter to her Lover, who communicated it, at our Deſire, to his Brethren. They importun'd us

from

Mr. JAMES M'EUEN,

S I R,

WE have at length, through the Interest and Means of the Honourable C. C——m Esquire, prevail'd with the Ladies of the Fair Intellectual-Club, to publish their Secretary's Letter, written to him some Months ago. Accordingly I have the Authority and Pleasure to convey the Manuscript, faithfully transcribed, to your Hand; that so rare a Patern and Example of Female Excellence may be no longer conceal'd, but set out to the View and Imitation of the less polite Part of that delicate Sex. Believe me to be with much Respect,

October 16
1719

S I R,

Your, &c.

from Time to Time, to allow the Publication of it, and, tho we were unwilling to deny or disoblige them, we consented with great Reluctancy. But now that it spreads, we resolve to discover our selves also very soon, provided we have the Pleasure to hear that others of our Sex have the Emulation to copy after our Example. Tho' we shou'd have been better pleas'd to continue in our belov'd Obscurity, we are neither asham'd to expose our Method of Procedure, nor our very Persons. And we hope the Opinion of Mankind concerning us shall not be lessened, when our Names and Conditions are more known. If we were not conscious to our selves of our Honesty, we shou'd dread the Consequences of this, much more of a greater or more publick Appearance. A good Disposition and Conscience preserve a constant Ease and Serenity within us, and will secure us from the Injuries of Calumny and Reproach. Besides, the ingenious *Gentlemen*, by whose Interest and Means our History comes to be published so soon, are too high in our Esteem not to be sufficient Judges and Vouchers of it. Their Approbation and Favour give abundance of Sanction to us; and we fear the Constructions of others the less, that we are invited to make our selves known by those whom we value, and who, we are sure, wou'd not advise us ill. If any condemn or pick Quarrels with us weaker Vessels,

from

[ ]

from whom no extraordinary great Things can be expected, we can't help accounting them ungenerous enough, especially considering this is our first Appearance, and a rare one too, as the Times go in this Nation. Ignorance of humane Nature, (whereof Women partake as well as Men) Malice, Weakness or Want of Thought, may occasion a great many Objections against us, such as, that we go out of our Sphere, that we neglect more proper Business, &c. but as it wou'd be folly to answer Libels before they are made, so to obviate these Objections here, wou'd be to alter the Purpose of this Advertisement.

We conclude in full Assurance, that Men of best Sense will be most favourable. As for those who have no just Title to that *Character*, we have no Reason, and as little Fancy to regard either their *Censure or Encomium*. We flatter our selves, the Males will not, but if any of our own Sex think fit to attack us, we hope to be able to give the World Satisfaction, while we put them to *Confusion* in *our Defences*

Vertue's defensive Armour must be strong,
To scape the merry and malicious Tongue.

D'AVEN.

Written and signed by { B. B. and M. D. } Members of the Club

AN
ACCOUNT
OF THE
Fair Intellectual - Club, &c.

SIR,

THE Intreaties of that *Honourable Society* where-of you are so deservedly a *Member*, have, with Difficulty, prevail'd on our CLUB, to let you into the Secret of its Original and present Constitution Accordingly, I am honoured by my SISTERS, to entertain you, with a brief Detail of the most considerable Circumstances, in our History. And, I own, 'tis with Vanity, as well as Pleasure, I have such a noble Occasion to write to a *Gentleman*, whose Merits I have long admir'd, and whose Friendship I justly value my self for Tho, at the same time, I have neither Assurance, nor

A   Skill

Skill enough, to support my *Character* in managing the Trust committed to me, whilst I address my self to one of your Judgment and Taste. But whatever my Weaknesses be, I know your Candour and Goodness will dispose you to be favourable, especially when you think of our Sex, and that particular Body I represent, in writing this Epistle

'Tis true, no Mistakes or Blunders I may be guilty of, either in Method, Sentiments, or Stile, can justly be imputed to my Constituents, who are concern'd no more than in giving Allowance and Command to write their History to you, who had the Cunning first to discover our Club, and therefore, I need not apologize for them   But I can't help thinking it a good Argument, to prevail with a fine Gentleman, who, on all proper Occasions, expresseth his Esteem and Regard for the *Ladies*, to pardon the natural Weaknesses of one for the Sake of the rest, to whom they are common

WITHOUT troubling you or my self with any other *Apology*, for the Rudeness that must certainly appear in the Composure of a Woman, so little accustomed to write, I shall proceed directly to the Purpose in Hand, and, as I can, afford you a just and impartial Account of that Club, which you are so fond to know.

YET, Sir, it will not be improper to notice in the *Preamble*, that, whatever Defects may happen in my Management of this Undertaking, no Person can pretend to understand the Thing better, or at least hath fairer Opportunities to know the Circumstances and State thereof, than I, who was one of the three *Ladies* that laid the Foundation of the Club, and have been preferred to be Miſtreſs *Secretary* of it, ever ſince its Eſtabliſhment, to the preſent Day. 'Tis in that Character I now write, however unworthy in Reſpect of ſome of my Siſters, who have conferred it upon me. And I beg the Privilege of being conſider'd as ſuch, whilſt you peruſe the following Relation

In the Month of *May* 1717, three young Ladies happened to divert our ſelves by walking in *Heriot's Gardens*, where one of us took Occaſion to propoſe that we ſhould enter into a Society, for Improvement of one another in the Study and Practice of ſuch Things, as might contribute moſt effectually to our Accompliſhment. This Overture ſhe enforc'd with a great deal of Reaſoning, that diſpos'd the other two cheerfully to comply with it. The Honour of our Sex in general, as well as our particular Intereſt, was intended, when we made that Agreement. We thought it a great Pity, that Women, who excell a great many others in *Birth* and *Fortune*, ſhould not alſo be more eminent in Virtue and good Senſe, which we might attain unto, if we were as induſtrious to cultivate our Minds, as we are to adorn our Bodies.

> 'Tis true that MAN is more ſublime and bold,
> But WOMAN's figur'd of a finer Mold
> Hence the ſoft Nature of her pliant Clay
> Will all Impreſſions take, all Forms obey
> Who then excludes the Virgin as unfit
> For the high Arts, and Myſteries of Wit?
> Or, why ſhould baſe, invidious Man deny
> The Search of Truth, to their diſcerning Eye?

Why, when ingenit Reason shoots her Ray
To light us all, are they forbid the Day?
Why should th'implanted Energy of Mind
Grow faint and flaken in the Female-Kind?
Imperial JOVE *forbids so great a Crime,*
Nor was APOLLO *only born to climb*
AONIAN *Hills, when to inhabit there,*
The MUSES *ever tuneful, ever fair.*
TRITONIAN PALLAS *does her* ÆGIS *weild,*
Nor Wit to PHOEBUS *or* GRADIVUS *yeild,*
But rules in ATHENS, *and commands the Field.,*

I presume, Sir, you'll excuse the Pedantry of this Quotation, which I remember to have read some where, in Honour of our Sex and in stead of Words, which I could not have used more fitly in Defence of the Design and Method we had agreed to pursue, for our mutual Improvement But in writing to you, I flatter my self, it is needless to insist in proving we are capable of a great many Arts and Vertues, that we too much neglect to Study and practise, neither need I mention the Reasons that determin'd us to make such a Transaction. The Hints already offered are sufficient to let an intelligent Person see, we neither go out of our Sphere, nor have acted inconsiderately in what we have done And more to the same Purpose may fall in naturally hereafter. In the mean Time, I shall proceed to tell you, That, according to our Paction, we resolved to meet in my Chamber on another Day, when, after Deliberation, we might concert Measures jointly for the Establishment of our CLUB When the appointed Time came, we met, and delivered by Turns, the Sentiments we had prepared be-

fore

fore hand by our felves. After much ferious Conference, 'twas concluded, That, neither a leffer nor greater Number than Nine fhould make up what we were to Name, *The* F A I R I N T E L - L E C T U A L - C L U B We were apprehenfive it would not be eafy to find out other Six, whofe Humours and Qualifications would render them every Way fit and agreeable Companions, in that Relation. However, we refolv'd to fpare no Pains in making a prudent Choice And in Order to maintain our wifhed for Harmony and Order, we immediately proceeded to adjuft fome Things among our felves, ere any more were invited to join us But finding it a Matter of great Importance to our C L U B, to have it well eftablifhed, we judged it expedient to adjourn our Meeting yet fome Days further, and, in the Interval have our Thoughts bufied, concerning what might be moft proper to be gone into, at our Meeting Each of us gave in a written Scheme of what we thought moft expedient to be agreed on, for the Regulation of the C L U B We reafoned on every Article propofed, and recorded, in a feparate Paper, whatfoever we gave mutual Affent unto Thus rejecting all the Overtures made by any of us, that were not approven and received by us all, we fixed on a few Articles, to which we unanimoufly agreed, on that Occafion Yet becaufe we were confcious of the Importance of the Tranfaction, it was judged requifite to adjourn till another Day, that we might be the more difpofed to fubfcribe to what was concluded before

Y o u muft have the Charity, Sir, to believe we were very ferious and deliberate in our Retirements, while we endeavoured to be fully fatisfied in our own Minds concerning the Reafonablencfs

and

and Expediency of what we were to do. The more Time we spent in thinking and conferring together upon the Meafures we had laid down, we were the more cheerfully difpofed to adhere to them ; in fo much that, when the Time of Meeting came, we were all ready to accomplifh our Defign, with the greateft Hope of Succefs and Expreffions of mutual Love and Friendfhip

THE Original of our CLUB being thus far fairly reprefented to you, Sir, it will not be thought unnatural in the next Place, to deliver the Contents of the Paper which we fubfcribed, upon the firft *Thurfday,* of *June,* and which I here tranfcribe from the Original it felf, as follows

✹✹✹✹✹✹✹✹✹✹✹✹✹✹✹✹✹✹✹✹✹✹✹✹✹✹✹✹✹✹
✹✹✹✹✹✹✹✹✹✹✹✹✹✹✹✹✹✹✹✹✹✹✹✹✹✹✹✹✹✹

The RULES *and* CONSTITUTIONS *of the* Fair INTELLECTUAL-CLUB *in* Edinburgh.

WE, whofe Names are underwritten, being fenfible of the Difadvantages that our Sex in General, and we in parti-cular labour under, for want of an eftablifhed Order and Method in our Converfation And being ambitious to imitate the lau-dable Example of fome of our Brethren, that make the greateft Figure in the learn'd and polite World, in fo far as we are capable and may reafonably be allowed, by entring into a mutual Com-pact and Agreement, to act for the Intereft and Improvement of one another, in our Meetings, have refolved to eftablifh a Club,

called,

called, *The* Fair-Intellectual-Club; and hereby declare our Assent, and Purpose to observe, (whilst we are alive and unmarried) *The* Rules *and* Constitutions, which follow;

I. That we shall maintain a sincere and constant mutual Friendship, while we live, and never directly nor indirectly reveal or make known, without Consent of the whole Club asked and given, the Names of the Members, or Nature of the Club.

II That none shall be invited or admitted into the Club before her Name be proposed in it, and her Merits impartially considered, and Allowance given by all the Members to have her introduced

III That none shall be declared a Member of our Club, before she hath, in our Presence, subscribed her Name to the Rules and Constitutions thereof

IV. That we shall never admit more than Nine into our Club, whereof Five shall be counted a *Quorum* sufficient to act in Absence of the rest, as if the Number was compleat.

V That none shall be invited or admitted into our Club before she be fifteen Years of Age, nor after her twentieth Year is expired

VI. That altho' different Principles and Politicks shall be no Hindrance to the Admission of Members into our Club,

being

being Proteftants Yet none fhall prefume to urge thefe directly or indirectly in our Meetings on Pain of Cenfure.

VII T H A T altho' we may, on proper Occafions, make Excurfions in Commendation of the Genius and Conduct of other People, yet none fhall be guilty of practifing the filly Arts of Cenfure and Ridicule, on Pain of Cenfure

VIII. T H A T every Perfon at her firft Admiffion into the C L U B, fhall entertain the C L U B with a written Harangue, and deliver the Sum of Ten Shillings *Sterling*, for the Ufe of the Poor, as we fhall direct

IX. T H A T one fhall be chofen at the Beginning of each Quarter of the Year, in our Meetings, to whom we fhall addrefs our felves when we fpeak, by the Name of *Miftrefs Speaker*, and pay all the due Refpect to her that becometh us to one, whom we impow'r to determine Differences, filence Debates, cenfure Tranfgreffors, ftate Votes, and in a Word, to perform all the Offices that one in the Character of P R E S E S may reafonably be allowed to do.

X T H A T *Miftrefs Speaker* fhall entertain the C L U B with a written Speech of her own Compofure, immediately before the Election of one to fucceed her in the Chair.

XI T H A T we fhall elect a Secretary to the Club, at the Beginning of each Quarter, immediately after the Choice of Mrs Speaker, and that fhe fhall record in a Book, and have the Cuftody of the Minutes of our Management, as of all other Papers prefented to the Club.

XII. T H A T Mrs. *Secretary* fhall read over the Minutes of all that pafs'd in the Club during her Quarter, immediately before the Election of one to fucceed her.

XIII. T H A T we fhall punctually attend on all the Meetings of our Club, which for ordinary are to be once a Week, and that Abfents fhall be cenfured, unlefs their Excufes be found to be good.

XIV. T H A T whofoever refufes to fubmit to the Command and Rebukes of the Club pronounced by Mrs. *Speaker*, fhall be expelled from it, if fober Reafoning can't prevail.

XV. T H A T when Death, Marriage, or other important Occurrences fhall, in the Courfe of Providence, remove any Member from our Club, Care fhall be taken to make a fpeedy Supply of her Room, left the Club fuffer, or go to nothing.

XVI. T H A T we fhall not be limited by our Subfcriptions from making new Regulations, Additions or Alterations, for our greater Good and Improvement, from Time to Time, as we fhall fee Caufe.

T H E S E Articles abovementioned were fubfcrib'd by us three, that compos'd them, before any were invited to join us. Two Weeks pafs'd ere we cou'd agree in the Choice of one to be a Member We thought we cou'd not be too cautious of admit-

ting

ting others into our Club, which we defign'd for fuch noble Purpo-
fes.   We were ambitious of a rational and felect Converfation,
compos'd of Perfons who have the Talent of pleafing with Delicacy of Sentiments flowing from habitual Chaftity of Thought
We were eager to keep out Pretenders to Mirth and Gallantry,
and all fuch who with conftrain'd, obfcene and painful Witti-
cifms, pefter People in mix'd Companies.   At Length we unanimoufly pitch'd on Three, whofe Genius and Conduct were moft
agreeable.   Thefe we endeavoured by feveral honeft Means to
gain.   The fix met, according to a Paction, in my Chamber,
where I, in Name of my Sifters, inform'd them of the Nature of
our Club, and read over the Rules and Conftitutions of it in their
Hearing, to which they cheerfully fubfcribed.   Now we had a
fufficient *Quorum*, and were capable to act, according to our
Rules, as we judg'd expedient.   A Day was appointed for our
Meeting, when we were alfo to chufe a *Speaker* and *Secretary*. But,
ere the Time came, we found a feventh Member to our unfpeak-
able Satisfaction.   Out of the Seven Mrs. *Speaker* and Mrs. *Secretary* were chofen.   You need not doubt, Sir, but we made a prudent Choice of Mrs. *Speaker*.   As for me, who had the Honour to
be made *Secretary*, I fhall not be fo proud as to appear fneakingly
Modeft, by running down my own Abilities for the fecond Poft in
our C L U B, which confifted meerly in a greater Dexterity in
Writing than the reft pretended to.   Mrs. *Speaker* being plac'd in
her Chair, and I at the Table, with proper Materials for the Dif-
charge of my Duty, the C L U B agreed that we fhou'd adjourn
our Meeting till the firft *Thurfday* of *July*, and in the Interval feek
out other two Ladies qualified to join us, and make our Number

com-

complete. As also, Mrs. *Speaker* was required to prepare a S P E E C H to be delivered by her at the opening of our grand Assembly. It happened very luckily, that before the first *Thursday of July* came, our C L U B was made up: Thus gradually are great Affairs brought to Perfection.

Y o u cannot imagine, Sir, the Joy we had when we found our selves conveened in the Character of Members of T H E F A I R I N T E L L E C T U A L-C L U B. For my Part I thought my Soul shou'd have leapt out of my Mouth, when I saw nine Ladies, like the nine *Muses*, so advantagiously posted. If ever I had a sensible Taste and Relish of true Pleasure in my Life, it was then. Oh! How delightful is the Pleasure of the Mind! None knows it but those who value Reason and good Improvement, above fine Shapes, Beauty and Apparel.

B u t to proceed, Sir, after some preliminary Things, such as the Admission of the two youngest Members, &c. Mrs. *Speaker* entertained us with a Speech, according to our Desire, and to our great Satisfaction. I believe you will be as fond to have a Copy of it, as to know the Circumstances hitherto related. And since I have obtain'd an unlimited Commission from the Club, I may venture to transcribe the Original, which is in my Hands at present. I do it the rather, because it will save me a great deal of Labour and Time, that I would otherwise be obliged to expend, in giving you a full Account of our present Constitution. From it, one of your discerning Judgment and Taste will easily learn our Conduct in our Meetings, and be able to determine, without a long Detail, whe-

ther

ther or not 'tis worth our while to keep up the Fair Intellectual-Club. Take it then Word for Word, as
followeth.

The Speech *of Mrs.* M——— Hamilton
Speaker of the Fair Intellectual-Club in *Edinburgh.*

Ladies,

I presume you will credit me, when I assure you, I was never
so much at a Loss all my Life for want of Abilities to express
the Sentiments of my Mind, as on this Occasion. When I consider in whose Company and in what Character I am at present,
my natural Vanity and Confidence fail me, and a dastard Fear
seizes on my Spirits Nor is it much to be wondered at, since I
appear before a Club of the most polite Ladies in *North-Britain,*
and attempt by your Commands to speak concerning an Establishment and Constitution, into which, contrary the Custom of
our Sex, we are entering, as adventurous Sailors into a new discovered Land. 'Tis my Pleasure however, that I know the Candor as
well as the Judgment of my Auditors, and that the Imperfections
of my Address can scarce exceed the Bounds of your Generosity.

Ladies,

We are here, by the good Conduct of divine Providence, as-
sembled in the Relation of Members of the same Body. The Society

ciety, in which we are engag'd, cannot be maintain'd without the most unfeign'd Friendship, and industrious Application. As mutual Love and Charity are necessary to preserve our Union and Harmony, so Diligence must be used in order to our Improvement in those Arts and Vertues, that may come under our Consideration. 'Tis our Accomplishment in every Thing our Sex may reasonably be allowed to study and practise, that we design'd by our late Transaction, and we can never, on good Grounds, hope to attain our desired End, unless we be sincerely engag'd in the common Interest. I do not mention this, as if I entertain'd the least Jealousy of your good Dispositions, after the Pains you have been at, to work your Minds to a cheerful Compliance with the Rules and Constitutions of the Club. But the Frailty of humane Nature gives abundance of Reason, to inculcate Things that are essentially necessary to the good Success of our Undertakings. Nor can it be unseasonable for us at any Time, to recommend what we are in so much Danger of forgetting, while we are furrounded with so many Temptations, and liable to so many Imperfections.

Order and Regularity in our Proceedings are so evidently requisite to our Success, that I don't know, if it would be consistent with Civility, if I should urge you, *Ladies*, to maintain them with the utmost Care. You have so well provided against the contrary, by your laudable Laws, that no Room is left to doubt but Matters will be carried on with the greatest Exactness and Decency. And the Light of natural Reason that shines illustriously in your whole Conduct, cannot miss to point out the Way to your

Interest,

Intereft, and difcover the Rocks on which you might otherwife ftumble. Give me Leave however to put you in Mind on this Occafion, that every Thing that appears good and ufeful in its felf, does not ly in the Road of our Improvement. A great many Things may be ftudied by the Male Sex, which, tho' we may alfo be capable to purfue them, don't properly concern us. Nor is it every Thing that may pleafe our own curious Fancies, that we fhou'd make the Subject of our Enquiries and Converfation. How apt are Women to trouble their Heads about nice Speculations and fubtile Difputes, they have no Intereft in? Let us not difcover fo much Weaknefs, as to prefer Out-of-the-Way-Things, to more folid and neceffary Entertainment. While we have fuch a glorious Body as the Sun before us, let us not feek Light from the Stars. When all that is neceffary to be known and done by us in our Sphere, is pofitive and certain, let us not vainly gaze at Shadows, and be delighted with probable Conjectures. And that we may keep clofs to our own Bufinefs, and give no juft Occafion to others, who may in Time become acquainted with our Management, to cenfure or ridicule us, allow me to unbofome my Thoughts to you, with all due Refpect and Submiffion to your fuperior Judgment and Difcretion, concerning the Things, which, in my Opinion, are properly our Concern.

LADIES,

IT may be thought ftrange if I fhould mention Religion and Vertue, in the firft Place, as neceffary Founations to our Society, and Things without which I defpair of Succefs in any of our Undertakings. And yet I cannot loofe fo fair an Opportunity of

declar-

declaring to you, whom I love fo dearly, that I look on the Study and Practice of thefe as abfolutely requifite, to render us great as well as good Women. I do not fay, that in Order to our attaining the Ends we have in View, we muft be joined to fuch and fuch a particular Sect of Chriftians, appear fo and fo grave and devout, put on an angry Zeal againft thofe who may be of a different Per-fwafion, or form to our felves the fame *Ideas* of Government or Policy. But I muft own it is my Sentiment, that true, unaffe-cted and unfophifticated Piety, a good Confcience toward God and Man, is the beft Bond of Society and Help to the obtaining a Bleffing on the Means we ufe to accomplifh our felves in other Matters. Nothing is fo kind and inviting as it is. It is fo far from impofing unneceffary Burdens on our Nature, that it eafeth us of the Weight, that our Paffions and Miftakes lay upon it. It is fo far from being always at Cuffs with good Humour, that it is unfeparably united therewith. Inftead of fubduing us with Ri-gour, it redeemeth us from the Slavery we are in to our felves, whilft we are under the Ufurpation of our Appetites let loofe and not reftrain'd. It is both the Foundation and Crown of all other Vertues. It cleanfeth the Underftanding, and brufheth off the Earth that hangeth about our Souls But why do I recommend this with fo much Warmth to you, who think it your Pleafure as well as your Duty and Intereft? You know well, it would be a vain Thing for you to direct your Behaviour in the World, and yet neglect that which you owe toward him that made it? If no Government can flourifh which does not encourage and propa-gate Religion and Morality among all its particular Members, fo our Society cannot ftand and profper without them. Befides, if

we

we are honeft and fincere in our Declarations of Friendfhip, and ambitious to promote the common Intereft, How can we chufe but to have a fpecial Regard to the facred Rule of Faith and Manners, in all our Conduct? Can we poffibly love and affift one another to propofe, and not fhew a tender Zeal for the Good and Happinefs of one another, in this and a future World? May the kindeft Influences of Heaven attend us in this Regard, and may no idle or lefs important Enquirys make us unmindful of what fo nearly concerneth us.

AND here, *Ladies*, I prefume to put you in Mind, that, whatever others think, we can never be out of Fafhion, while we are bold and open in the Profeffion and Practice of all Chriftian Duties. All People who have not caft off all Principles of Fear and Hope, are ferious and attentive to the great Bufinefs of their Being. Religious Motives and Inftincts are fo very bufy in the Heart of every reafonable Creature, that whofoever would hope to govern a Society without any Regard to thefe Principles, is as much to be contemn'd for Folly, as detefted for Impiety Let us endeavour to maintain a due Veneration for the fupreme Being in our whole Conduct, and obferve ftrictly the Rules of Morality in our Dealings with one another, and with all the World. To thefe Ends it is of high Importance to perufe the facred Scriptures often, and with utmoft Attention, particularly the *Pfalms* of *David*, that beft Pattern and Help to Devotion And *Solomon*'s *Proverbs* the beft Syftem of Morality the World was ever bleft with. Nor can we be fo wanting to our own Duty, Pleafure and Improvement, as to neglect the Study of the New Teftament in a

fpe-

fpecial Manner fince in thofe ineftimable Writings are lodged all the Treafures of divine Knowledge and the Words of eternal Life. The beft Way will be to make them the firft and laft of all our Studies, to open and clofe the Day with that facred Book, wherein we have a faithful and moft entertaining Hiftory of that bleffed and miraculous Work of the Redemption of the World, and fure Directions how to qualify and entitle our felves for the great Salvation purchafed by *Jefus.* This Exercife will compofe our Thoughts into the fweeteft Serenity and Chearfulnefs, and happily confecrate all our Time and Studies to G o D.

B u t, *Ladies,* tho' a fteddy Courfe of good Life, running like a fmooth Stream, fhould be a perpetual Spring to furnifh us to the continued Exercife of Vertue, tho' we fhould live in the World, fo as it may hang about us like a loofe Garment, yet we are not tied up from making Enquiries into fuch other Things as may improve our Minds in ufeful Knowledge, and render us exemplary to all who obferve our Conduct. 'Tis requifite we fhou'd alfo, with due Dependance on the divine Bleffing, read proper Books in our refpective Abodes. Tho' the Circumftances of Life make thefe lefs our Study, than of the Male Sex, yet the Propenfity we find in our Natures to read, and the Improvements fome of our Kind have made by Study, may fatisfy us that it is an Injuftice to deprive us of thofe Means of Knowledge. How elfe fhall we exprefs our Fondnefs to have our Natures reform'd, and refute thefe fcandalous Afperfions caft upon our Sex, that we are made up of Pride, Affectation, Inconftancy, Falfhood, Treachery, Tyranny, Luft, Ambition, Wantonnefs, Levity, Difguife,

Coquetry,

Coquetry, and the like ill Things, so often in the Mouths and Writings of Men? For my Part, *Ladies*, I think the safest and surest Way of Gainsaying such light Accounts of our Sex, is to think them all Truths, till we can work up our own Minds and Practice to such a Pitch of Greatness, as we may look down with Pity on the vu'gar Mistakes concerning us. Let us endeavour to attain such Habits and Dispositions of Soul, as cannot be justly censured, till we arrive that Length, I don't see how we can be secured from Raillery, or yet offended at it Accordingly our Studies shou'd chiefly be such, as lead to Rectitude of Mind and Life. And if I were to name proper Books for that Purpose, I I cou'd not make a better Choice than, I believe, all of you have already done in reading *The whole Duty of Man, Bishop Tillotson's Sermons, Charon on Wisdom, The Tatler, Spectator, Guardian, Lady's Library, Hallifax's Advice to a Daughter, Reflections on Ridicule, The Gentleman instructed, Lucas on Happiness*, and the like. These are of constant and universal Use to form the Mind, and direct us in all the Relations of Life that do now, or may possibly concern us, as Women and Christians And how useful and entertaining will it be for us frequently to converse in our Meetings, on Subjects concerning which we have read in our Retirements!

BUT, *Ladies*, we have yet more Work on our Hands. And by the By, we may observe how little of our Time shou'd be spent in Idleness, which too many of our Sex think themselves indulged in, on the Account of their Softness and Delicacy. But alas! must we think we have nothing to do, because we can do nothing? Shall we complain of Inabilities, when we are at no

Pains to be able to perform? Let other Women think what they will, in my Opinion, an idle one is a Monster in the Creation. All Nature is busy about us, Every Animal we see reproaches Want of Industry. How inexcusable are they, who have a greater Variety of Business, to which they may apply themselves, than the Brutes? Reason opens to us a large Field of Affairs, which other Creatures are not capable of. Alas! That any of our Species, shou'd at any Time complain that the Day hangs heavy upon them, that they do not know what to do with themselves, that they are at a Loss how to pass away their Time. How monstrous are such Expressions among Creatures, who have the Labours of the Mind, as well as those of the Body, to furnish them with proper Employments? Who, besides their little Family Affairs, can apply themselves to the Duties of Religion, to Meditation, to the Reading of useful Books, to Discourse, in a Word, who may exercise themselves in the unbounded Pursuits of Knowledge and Vertue, and every Hour of their Lives make themselves wiser or better than they were before. But when I remember I am speaking to you, *Ladies,* my Weakness is check'd and my Incivility reprov'd. I know you have nothing more than Want of Industry and Sloth. 'Tis to your extraordinary Diligence and Application that all that Progress and Advancement you have made in Female Accomplishments, are owing. I believe I carry the Commendation no further than it should be, when I say, that by your Diligence you understand History, Geography, Arithmetick and such like Businesses, so useful in Life, as well as any of your Sex. Nor do you confine your Studies so much, as to neglect the *French* and *Italian* Languages, which are

accounted

accounted so polite and fashionable in this Age. But when I consider the Improvements all of you have made in the *English* Language, I can never cease to admire your Judgment and Application. As nothing less than a right Taste of the Excellency and Beauty of Writing and Speaking well, could determine you to be at due Pains to attain them; so, without great Industry and Application, it had been impossible for you to have become Mistresses of the *English* Language in such Perfection, especially considering, how difficult it is for our Country People to acquire it. And here I cannot cease to reflect with Indignation on the Negligence of our Sex, in this Particular. What a Shame is it, that *Ladies* who value themselves for Wit and Politeness, shou'd yet be ignorant of their Mother Tongue? How many set up for Wits, that can't write good Sense, in proper Language? And how few can pronounce what they read, or deliver themselves, with a proper Grace? The more trivial these Faults appear, the greater Reproach to those who cannot correct them. Few, very few of the *Ladies* I have had Occasion to know, can so much as spell. Good God! What have they to boast of? How can they censure others with the least Assurance, who can scarce do any Thing to Purpose themselves? Pardon me then, *Ladies*, tho' I gratefully acknowledge my Duty to Heaven and you, on this Occasion, for the Privilege of being admitted to share the Blessings of your Conversation, who have distinguished your selves from the common Herd of Women, by your Diligence to acquire such admirable Qualities as you now possess.

A N D here, *Ladies*, I think it a natural Transition also to celebrate the Bounty and Goodness of the Almighty God in your Behalf, who has furnished you so richly with Genius's capable of the most sublime and refin'd Arts ; nor does it derogate from the Gratitude and Duty we owe to the supreme Being and Author of these Talents you possess, to praise you for the Diligence you have used to improve them. You have in great Measure perfected what Nature began , particularly, you have made such Improvements in the Sister Arts of *Poetry*, *Musick* and *Painting*, for which your Genius's seem to have been design'd, that few, if any of our Sex, in this Kingdom, excel you in these Accomplishments. Here I might take Occasion to discourse at some Length in your Hearing, concerning these noble Arts you are so fond to cultivate and practise in our Club. I might make Excursions in their Praise, and by many Arguments enforce the Study of them. But, as I apprehend, you are in no such Danger of neglecting them, as of being too curious and painful in your Enquiries that Way. I shall only with due Submission and Respect, represent to you the Danger of employing too much of your Time about them. And while I discourse concerning them, I wou'd be understood to speak what I know by Experience. I own it, my Genius and Fancy have been so bent upon some one or other of them at different Times, that I have been frequently indisposed for any Thing else. I have often been tempted by their alluring Charms, to postpone my Duty to G o d and my Neighbour, to the Gratification of my own Humour. To begin with *Poetry*, (which indeed uses not to be the Temptation of too many of our *Scots Ladies*) What Variety of Charms are in it, to captivate our Minds. Great, inspiring

great is its Ufe in humane Life.   But alas! There is fo much
Enchantment, fo much Poifon under a gilded Cover, that
none fhould be trufted with it, who want abundance of Judgment and Tafte.   The very reading, much more the compofing
is dangerous.   There is, I know not what in it, that infenfibly
leadeth the Heart to Love, Idlenefs and Frenzy.   But I would
not be underftood, as if I meant all Sorts of Poetry were equally
dangerous.   Divine and moral Poetry I wou'd urge with all my
Reafon and Rhetorick.   'Tis the Hazard of reading and compofing foft and wanton Works, that warm and corrupt the Imagina-
tion, I chiefly intend   We cannot be too careful in the Choice of
Authors and Subjects.   Every Poem and every Theme is not for
common Hands.   Even thofe who have a very good Judgment and
Tafte are in Hazard, while they deal in fuch Poetry, as is not re-
trench'd and purify'd from whatfoever tends to the corrupting of
the Soul.   Such Poems as anfwer the original Ends of it, *viz.* to
excite in the Soul lively and fublime Notions of G o d and Religion, may be ufed with Delight and Freedom   Next to the *Pfalms*
of *David*, and other poetical Parts of *Holy-Write*, We have nothing in our *Englifh* Language that I efteem comparable to the
Writings of Sir *Richard Blackmore*, Mr. *Ifaac Watts*, and Doctor
Young.   There is alfo a *Collection of divine Hymns and Poems*, done
by eminent Hands, and publifhed by Mrs. *Singer*, which I great-
ly admire.   There are many good Performances in *Dryden's Mif-
cellanies*, and other Collections and Works, which I can fcarce
venture to recommend, while they are in fuch bad Company.
But to you I need not be affraid to recommend the Writings of
Milton, *Cowley* and *Norris*. Comedies fhould be read with Caution,
and

and few of them at all · But Tragedies, well wrought, are highly
to be priz'd, and ſtudied. Yet I have not ſo much Vanity as to
pick and chuſe out of them a Liſt of the beſt and moſt uſeful. I
ſhall only tell you, as I have done all along, my private Sentiments with Freedom and Submiſſion. I have ſeen none in *Engliſh*
that I like better than *Shakeſpear's*, *Ottway's* and *Row's*. I pretend
not to underſtand the Rules exactly, but I may be allowed to
know my own Nature, and to approve moſt what works on it beſt.
But 'tis Time now to vary my Subject, and I believe, *Ladies*, you
may gueſs from what I have ſaid concerning *Poetry*, what Regulations I cou'd wiſh to have in the Buſineſs of *Muſick* and *Painting*.
The Fancy is oft too quick in them, and the Soul too much affe-
cted by the Senſes. I ſpeak it from Experience, when I ſay *Muſick*
in a ſpecial Manner enervates and expoſes it to be conquered by
the firſt Temptation that invades it Pity it is that ſo many
Hours ſhou'd be ſquandered away on Sounds, and that we ſhou'd
take ſo much Pleaſure in gratifying a Senſe that has ſo often pro-
ven a Traytor to Vertue. If a chriſtian Turn was given to it, it
wou'd be, like *Poetry*, the greateſt Help to diſreliſh profane Plea-
ſures, and elevate the Mind. And as for *Painting*, for which
few have a Genius, I ſhall only ſay, it is no leſs a Pity that ſo
much Time ſhou'd be ſpent in teaching a young Lady to draw a
Flower, or paint on a Glaſs, *&c.* which ſhou'd be employed in
forming the Mind to Vertue, and the moral Duties of Life But
ye who underſtand the Principles of it, know well enough how
to manage your ſelves concerning it. As you can give that Variety and Beauty, that Regularity and Grace to your Pictures, which
can only make them valuable, ſo you can order your Time ſo the
ſeaſonable Entertainment, L

LADIES,

I flatter my self you conceive well enough the Design I have in making such particular Reflections concerning the three *Sister-Arts* on this Occasion: And perhaps I shou'd not have gone so far out of the common Way of thinking and judging now in Fashion among our Ladies of Wit and Gallantry, if I were not conscious of the great Danger we are in, of carrying them to Extremes; and consequently, of suffering more Hurt, than of gaining Advantage by our Enquiries and Diversion that Way. I shall now conclude ere you are quite wearied and disgusted with my Discourse. Only I beg Leave to put you in Mind, that our future Comfort and Success in our Club, must arise out of the happy Methods we fall upon at its Commencement. May the Almighty favour our Undertakings, and crown our Endeavours with such Fruits, as may render us useful not only to our selves, but to all we are concern'd in, and exemplary to our whole Sex in these, and succeeding Times.

THUS, Sir, I have presented you with an exact Transcript of the Speech our Mrs. *Speaker* delivered at the Establishment of the FAIR INTELLECTUAL CLUB. I leave you to judge, whether or not the Author of it deserv'd the Chair. She has since owned to us, that, having but little Time to compose it, and a great many Things in her Head, she was oblig'd to hudle up what occur'd to her very indistinctly, and forgot some Things that might as properly have been observ'd on that Occasion. But from it you may guess what her Genius and Disposition are. And

you

you will, I hope, be so charitabe as to believe, we have been to this Day as careful to maintain good Order in our Meetings, as she has appear'd zealous in recommending it.

But to go on with my History ; it is natural in the next Place to tell you, Sir, that after the forementioned Speech was delivered, Work was contriv'd for every Member, as the Club found expedient. All the Minutes of our Procedure are in my Hand at present But it will be needless to record them in this Epistle. And I suppose you have already form'd just Ideas of our Manage-. ment, from what has been presented to you. In a Word, we have carefully obferv'd our Rules hitherto, and made some new Regulations, as we found Caufe. All the *Speeches, Poems, Pictures,* &c. done by any Member, from that to this Day, are carefully kept. I have also by me an Index of the very Subjects of our Converfation all along, to which you, Sir, or any *Member* of your honourable *Society* may have Accefs at Pleafure. And for this Reafon, I shall omit a great many Things that might be reckoned confiderable and entertaining in this Account. There is one Speech however made by a young *Lady,* who was last admitted into our Club, in Room of another remov'd out of it, by a Husband, which I have the Vanity to tranfcribe from the Original, for your Entertainment. I own I was extremely fond of it, when it was delivered. But the chief Reafon why I trouble you with a Copy of it, is, that you may be helped to form an Idea of the Nature and Method of Difcourfes, delivered by Members at their Admiffion into the Club. Take it then as followeth.

The

The SPEECH *of Mrs.* M---- B----
Upon her Admission into the *Fair Intellectual-Club.*

LADIES,

THE Honour this Day conferr'd upon me is so great, so extraordinary and unexpected, that whilst I return my most grateful Acknowledgments, I am almost doubtful if I ought to believe it When I reflect on my own Inabilities and Unfitness to answer the Ends of a *Member* of this illustrious *Society*, I find so many Reasons appearing against my Admission, that, I am at once surpriz'd at your Goodness, and ashamed to present my Person. Can I have the Vanity to imagine I am judg'd worthy to join you in this Establishment? Can I believe you have not receeded from the essential Laws and Maxims you have formerly maintain'd in receiving new Members? Are not all Persons excluded this your Communion, who are not possest of a spotless Vertue, an extraordinary Wit, and comparable even to you? And how much a Stranger to my self must I be, if I am not conscious I have too little just Claim and Pretension to the *Character* a *Lady* shou'd necessarly have before she be made one of the INTELLECTUAL-CLUB?

I know very well, *Ladies*, that in the Choice you make of Persons to supply your vacant Seats, you have no Regard to the

the precarious Dignities of *Birth* and *Fortune*; that *Vertue*, *Breeding*, a good *Genius* and Acquaintance with the more gentle and polite *Arts*, have always ushered in naked Merit to you. And that you do not think it is below you to substitute in the Room of a noble *Lady*, lately remov'd from your Society, some Woman of a meaner Condition, whom her Genius and Conduct have rendered illustrious. But if you barely consider me, as a Person of this Sort, what can I offer you that may be worthy of the Favour with which you have been pleased to honour me? Is it a wretched Copy of Verses, commendable rather on the Account of my Boldness in composing them, than for the Beauty of their Thoughts, or the Richness of their Language? Is it because I have a tolerable Ear for *Musick*, and can play on a *Spinet* or *Flute*, to the Diversion of my partial Friends? Or is it because I can blend Colours, imitate a Draught, and make up a silly Figure by my Pencil? No, *Ladies*, you are too 'well acquainted with the just Value of Thingss to recompense at so high a Rate, such low Productions as mine, as to offer me upon so slight a Foundation, an Honour which the Knowledge of my Want of Abilities and Merit make me ashamed to take?

WHAT can then be the Reason which in my Behalf, has so happily influenc'd you, on this Occasion? I begin now to discover it, and I dare say, I am in the Right. Your Generosity and Disposition to encourage and improve the first Dawnings of Merit and Inclinations towards it, wherever you can find them in a Person, who, you think will at least reckon her self under eternal Obligations to you, and ready to obey your Commands to the ut-

most

moft of her Power. This I take to be the Occafion of that
Choice you have made of me   Your Goodnefs and Charity have
put you on a Method to try my Refpect and Gratitude. With the
Mein of a Requeft you have commanded me, and with the
Afpect of receiving a Favour you have oblig'd me to be for ever
grateful and obedient.   And I hope I fhall never give you Occafion to repent of the Choice you have made on that Score.   Happy
fhall I be, if by my Refpects and fincere Submiffions, I can perfectly
convince you of the extreme Acknowledgment which I fhall
make all my Days for the unexpected Honour you have done me.
Happy if my Attendance upon you, by my Addrefs in bringing
you to converfe about the moft ufeful Things, I can engage you
to conceal nothing of all your Knowledge and Skill, from me

AND here, *Ladies*, I muft be allowed to tell you, what Ideas
I have form'd of your *Club*, and what Advantages I have pro-
mifed my felf, by a diligent Attendance upon it.   I think I fee
my felf happily plac'd in the Company of *Ladies*, who, as they
are exalted above me, in Refpect of Birth and Fortune, are alfo
far my Superiors in the Accomplifhments of Female Life.   'Tis
not my Purpofe, and I think it wou'd be naufeous Entertainment
to you, to launch forth in Commendation of your Beauty, your
Airs, Shapes, Mein and other external Confiderations, which
might as juftly be the Subject of a *Panegyrick*, as thefe of any o-
ther in the Kingdom.   I leave Excurfions of that Nature to your
humble Servants of the Male Sex, who, if they have Difcretion,
cannot fail to celebrate your Perfections, and, if they have Wit
enough, will give you more Commendation than you wou'd de-
fire

fire to have or hear. But I beg Leave to fay in the general, that, as Beauty and Vertue meet in you in a wonderful Perfection, fo, as their Nature is, they mutually affift each other, Your Beauties are the more illuftrious, that you are vertuous: Yea, your very Piety and Religion receive a Prevalency, as well as a Luftre, from the Elegancy of your Meins and the Gracefulnefs of your Perfons. When that which is lovely, joins with that which is good, the firft makes Intereft with our Senfes for the Admiffion of the laft, and the latter calls in the Affiftance of our Reafon to embrace the former. Thus it has happened, that, fome have fixed their Eyes on a fair Example of Piety, to an utter Deteftation of Vices, and gaz'd themfelves into a Newnefs of Life. 'Tis an excellent Obfervation I remember to have read fome where, " That to behold a Perfon only vertuous, ftirs in us a prudent Re- " grate, to behold a Perfon only amiable to the Sight, warms us " with a religious Indignation , but to turn our Eyes on one poffeft " of both thefe Qualifications, gives us Pleafure and Improvement. " It works a Sort of Miracle, occafions the Byafs of our Nature to " fall off from Sin, and makes our very Senfes and Affections Con- " verts to Religion, and Promotters of our Intereft. Now, *Ladies*, if fuch noble Effects may be produced in thefe, who, at a Diftance behold and wonder at your Charms, what bleft Advantages may I not promife to my felf, who am to be fo happy as to be your conftant Companion? There is an Obfervation in *Holy-Writ*, which I may mention with Integrity on this Occafion, becaufe it is fo pertinent to my own Cafe. It is fpoken by the Queen of *Sheba*, when fhe faw the Wifdom of *Solomon· Happy are thy Men, happy are thefe thy Servants, who ftand continually before thee, and who hear thy Wifdom.*

BUT

But, *Ladies*, besides the Advantages I shall receive by a diligent Observation of your Vertue and Beauty; I think I see my self improven in all the *Sister Arts* of *Poetry*, *Musick* and *Painting*, in writing and speaking well; and, in a Word, in all the various Businesses of Female-Life, that may be requisite to come under your Consideration. How can I miss to be thus accomplished, if I be not mine own Enemy, whilst I enjoy the Friendship and Assistance of the Fair Intellectual-Club? A *Club*, that more than the Body regards the Mind, and prefers Substances to Shadows and Things that cannot profit. A *Club*, that pities these whose high Descent, whose Out-Side makes up all the Fame they know and vainly boast of. A *Club* that knows the true Value and Use of Things, is above the Reach of Envy, and secure of the fairest Character. A *Club* whose Glory is to pity, pardon and commend, but too great and good to ridicule, censure and disdain In a Word, a *Club* whose Match I dispair to hear of or know, till I join the innumerable Company of Angels and Society of Saints, arriv'd at consummate Perfection.

This, *Sir*, was the Speech I valued so much, not merely on the Account of the *Panegyrick* the *Lady* was pleased to make upon our *Club*, but also, for the genteel Matter it contains, and the graceful Manner of her Delivery, which last cannot be presented to you in Paper. She says the Beginning of it is an aukward Translation of *Boileau's* Speech at his Admission into the *French Academy*, which she was oblig'd to have Recourse to, because she had but a Day's Time to prepare one. I own it is an Imitation of

that

that great *Monfieur*'s Speech on that Occafion, but when you have compared the two, I cou'd almoft engage, you'll determine in the *Lady's* Favour, all Circumftances being rightly confidered.

Now, *Sir*, as I doubt not but you are wearied with the Account already given, fo I affure you I am heartily fatigued, and my Pen is quite ufelefs. Yet ere I conclude the Epiftle, I cannot forget to infoim you of an Overture made by the Author of the precceding Speech, and now fram'd into a Law by the C l u b, *viz.* That at every Meeting a Difcourfe fhall be delivered on fome Subject, according to the Direction and Appointment of the C l u b. And that each Member fhall have it by Turns, fufficient Time being allowed them for Preparation thereof. In Purfuance of this Refolution, we have agreed to harangue by Turns on the moral Vertues, and their oppofite Vices in the firft Place. And next, to enter on particular Subjects of *Poetry, Mufick, Painting, Wit, Breeding, Gallantry, Honour, Games, The Fafhions, &c.* We think Difcourfes on the Subjects concerning which we are to converfe in our Meetings, aie proper Introductions to what we fay by Word of Mouth. When one of us has duly confidered the Subject, and harangued upon it, we will be fitter to talk at greater Length for our Improvement, befides, we have refolved to make particular *Criticifms* on the Beauties and Imperfections of every Difcouife delivered on fuch Occafions, and to preferve them all in the Hands of Mrs. *Secretary*, that our Succeffois or other Perfons indulg'd by our C l u b, may have the Pleafuie to peiufe them.

Y o u may eafily difcern, *Sir*, that I have pafs'd over very confiderable Things in our Hiftory. But the Account I have given you, will enable you, as I faid before, to judge and determine concerning us. We fhou'd be proud to be approven by you. As no Perfon who has not been, or is a Member of our C L U B, is privy to our Management, except your felf and your honourable Brethren of an *Athenian Society*, fo I conjure you to let none elfe into the Secret, by expofing this Letter, or otherwife, without Confent of our C L U B. We are not afraid of Reproach or Cenfure, tho' our Conduct was made publick, and our Perfons known to the World? But by our Laws we are bound to maintain Secrefy, till all of us are willing to be known, which I do not expect you will entreat of us fo foon

I conclude with giving you the agreeable Affurance of our C L U B's unfeign'd Refpect to yours, and particularly to your felf, whofe *Genius* and Conduct they have been inform'd of, by,

Edinburgh, Jun
28th, 1719

S i r,

Your moft obedient, and

moft humble Servant,

M. C.

CPSIA information can be obtained at www.ICGtesting.com
Printed in the USA
BVOW10s1155220714

360054BV00023B/821/P

The Successful Softw Manager

The definitive guide to growing from developer to manager

Herman Fung

BIRMINGHAM - MUMBAI

The Successful Software Manager

Acquisition Editor: Andrew Waldron
Acquisition Editor - Peer Reviews: Suresh Jain
Project Editor: Tom Jacob
Development Editor: Alex Sorrentino
Copy Editor: Safis Editing
Technical Editor: Aniket Shetty
Proofreader: Safis Editing
Indexer: Tejal Daruwale Soni
Graphics: Sandip Tadge
Production Coordinator: Sandip Tadge

First published: June 2019

Production reference: 1270619

Published by Packt Publishing Ltd.
Livery Place
35 Livery Street
Birmingham
B3 2PB, UK.

ISBN 978-1-78961-553-1

www.packtpub.com